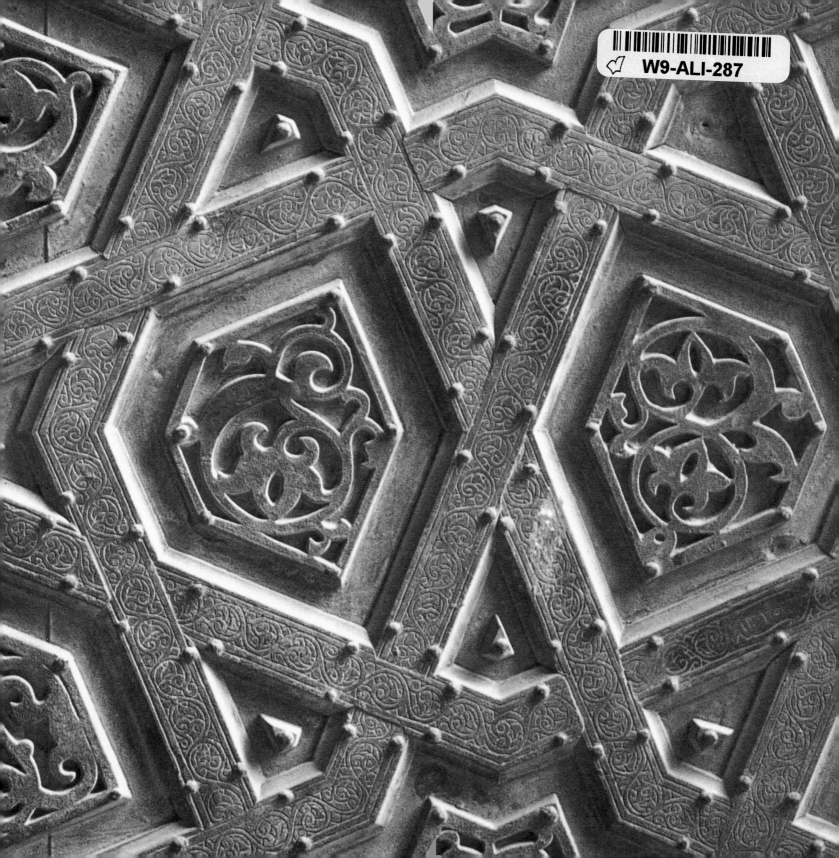

Cats of Cairo

Cats of Cairo

EGYPT'S ENDURING LEGACY

Lorraine Chittock

INTRODUCTION BY
Dr. Annemarie Schimmel

ABBEVILLE PRESS PUBLISHERS
New York London Paris

Domesticated animals are our link with the wild.
Let our gift to them be respect and reverence.

COVER: *Mosque of al'Mu'ayyad near Bab Zuwayla*
FRONTISPIECE: *Opposite the Mosque of Qajamas al-Ishaqi, Darb al-Ahmar*
TITLE PAGE: *Inside of the Mosque of al-Mu'ayyad near Bab Zuwayla*

Photographs © 1999 by Lorraine Chittock;
lorrainechittock@bigfoot.com
Introduction © 1999 by Dr. Annemarie Schimmel

Ancient Egyptian translations:
Jaromir Malek: page numbers 13, 14, 19, 22, 25, 26, 93.
Dr. M. Depauw: page numbers 16, 20.

Excerpt from 'The Tavern of the Black Cat,' by Naguib Mahfouz,
reprinted by permission of
The American University in Cairo Press.
Motifs from *Ancient Egyptian Patterns* and *Islamic Designs,* by Eva Wilson,
published by The British Museum Press, 1997.
'Envy' and 'Every Cat Has a Story' printed by permission of the author,
Naomi Shihab Nye. 'Envy' first appeared in *Hugging the Jukebox,* published
by E.P. Dutton; 'Every Cat Has a Story' first appeared in *English Journal.*
'After Fever' printed by permission of the author, Lisa Suhair Majaj.

'The Gayer Anderson Cat,' EA 64391 page 7, printed
by courtesy of the Trustees of the British Museum.
'The gnawing mouse,' page 9, MS Poc 400 fol (cat), and
'The married man and his family,' page 10, MS Bodl Or133 fol 40r,
by courtesy of the Bodleian Library.

The publisher is grateful for permission to reproduce material.
While every reasonable effort has been made to trace copyright holders,
the publisher would be pleased to hear from any not here acknowledged.

Designer: Patty Fabricant
Production Director: Louise Kurtz
Editor: Ashley Benning

First Published by Camel Caravan Press
© 2000 Abbeville Press, New York

2 4 6 8 10 9 7 5 3 1

Library of Congress Cataloging-in-Publication Data
Chittock, Lorraine, 1960–
Cats of cairo:Egypt's enduring legacy/Lorraine Chittock;
introduction by Annemarie Schimmel.
p. cm.
ISBN 0-7892-0707-9
1. Cats—Egypt—Cairo. I. Title.

SF442.63.E3 C45 2001
636.8'00962'16—dc21   00-05185

Acknowledgments

John Dawson, a reluctant cat lover, who listened endlessly, patiently, and lovingly while watching this book proceed. Thank you for meticulous editing and counsel on so many aspects of this project.

Dick Doughty, for making valuable time to assist with the book's flow from both a visual and literary viewpoint. Thank you for your inspired and knowledgeable editing.

Dr. Annemarie Schimmel, for freely sharing valuable information accumulated during years of dedicated scholarship. A precious gift of knowledge from one cat lover to another.

Jaromir Malek, whose academic knowledge of Egyptology and love of cats were indispensible for this project's completion.

Dr. M. Depauw for demotic translations.

Liz Waygood for translation.

Andrea Pape-Christiansen for endless hours of intuitive and sensitive translation.

Professor Yahya Michot at the Oxford Centre for Islamic Studies for research assistance.

Sally Skerrett for thoughtful design assistance on numerous occasions.

Ahmed Sultan for his beautiful cat calligraphy.

Matthew Kleinosky for patiently putting together a long overdue website.

Linda Cox, for her invaluable coordination after I'd left Cairo and warm welcome when I returned.

Neil Hewison, who was always willing to share information.

Andy Smart for the camaraderie and support of a fellow publisher.

Mike and Kelly Zaug, who gave me confidence in this book.

Tanya Watkins (British Museum) and Doris Nicholson (Bodleian Library) for picture research.

My mother, Barbara Timms, for all the cat books you lovingly gave me as a child.

And especially to all the cat lovers in Cairo who enthusiastically shared their love of cats with me.

Introduction

by Annemarie Schimmel

When the British orientalist E. W. Lane lived in Cairo in the 1830s he was quite amazed to see, every afternoon, a great number of cats gathering in the garden of the High Court, where people would bring baskets full of food for them. In this way, he was told, the *qadi* (judge) fulfilled obligations dating from the thirteenth-century rule of the Mamluk sultan al-Zahir Baybars. This cat-loving monarch had endowed a "cats' garden," a pious foundation where the cats of Cairo would find everything they needed and liked. In the course of time the place had been sold and resold, changed and rebuilt; yet the law required that the sultan's endowment should be honored, and who better than the *qadi* to execute the king's will and take care of the cats?

The tradition continues. To this very day, every visitor to the Islamic world is aware of the innumerable cats in the streets of Cairo—and of Istanbul, Kairouan, Damascus, and many other cities. Virtually everywhere, one is reminded of the saying popularly attributed to the Prophet Muhammad: "Love of cats is part of the faith."

Yet of all Middle Eastern cities, it is still Cairo where cats seem to be most beloved, for here the traditions regarding cats long predate Islam. In ancient Egypt the cat was among the most important deities: the highest god, Ra, was sometimes addressed as "Supreme Tomcat," and in the 'Book of the Dead,' which dates to the second millennium B.C., the cat was also equated with the sun—when we admire the slim, golden Nubian cats we can well understand this!

The bronze 'Gayer-Anderson cat' (c. 664-630 B.C.), British Museum

Legend tells that in times immemorial the sun-god Ra, in the shape of an enormous cat, fought against and overcame darkness manifesting itself as a powerful serpent.

Thus it is perhaps not too surprising that this ancient myth of the cat of light and the snake of darkness appears in a different guise millennia later in the Islamic world. According to one folktale, a snake came one day to the Prophet Muhammad to ask him a favor, but instead of thanking him it curled itself around his waist and was on the point of biting him when a friend of his passed by. This pious man was called Abu Hurayra, "Father of the kitten," as he always carried his cat with him in a bag. Seeing the beloved Prophet endangered, he opened his bag and let the cat out. She immediately attacked the snake and killed it, thus rescuing the Prophet from his enemy. Gratefully the Prophet stroked her back, which is why cats never fall on their backs; and he touched her head, and so every cat has four little stripes on her forehead—the marks of the Prophet's fingers.

In ancient Egypt people worshiped not only the lion-headed goddess Sekhmet but, more importantly, the gentler cat-headed Bastet, whose temple was located in Bubastis in the Nile Delta. Here, special priests devoted themselves to the cat's services, living there according to a strict code of behavior.

We do not know at which point in history the Egyptians succeeded in taming cats. They may have discovered them in Nubia where the cat is still regarded as a bearer of good luck. Soon they must have found out how useful these animals were: who else would have been able to kill, or at least to scare away, the mice that threatened the greatest wealth of ancient Egypt, the grain stored in the granaries? It follows almost naturally that the first story about the war between cats and mice originated in ancient Egypt, and was told and retold all over the world in poetry and in prose.

A cat today in the Mosque of al-Mu'ayyad near Bab Zuwayla, Cairo

7

The ancient Egyptians did everything to make their cats happy: they were groomed and bathed, anointed with fragrant oils, and of course fed with excellent food. For a cat's life was considered as important as a human life, and even during famines some food was apportioned to cats. And who would have dared to eat a cat, as was done so often in Europe in times of famine, when the poor creature might appear on the dinner plate under the name of "roof rabbit?" In Egypt, it was not unknown for someone who killed a cat to be executed or, if he happened to be caught in the act, lynched by the furious masses. The life of a cat has always been considered precious throughout the Islamic world: in Turkey it has been thought that even to build a mosque was not sufficient to atone for the killing of a cat, and in Muslim Bengal only eleven pounds of the most precious commodity, salt, was acceptable blood money for the death of a cat. In other regions the dead cat was hung by her tail, and the culprit had to heap grains around the animal until not even the tip of the tail remained visible.

Naturally, even in Egypt the beloved pets had to die at some point. The death of a cat was a cause of tremendous grief for the owner who, if his wealth allowed it, would embalm the animal and wrap it in fine linen perfumed with cedar oil. Great cat funerals took place in Bubastis: they were solemn ceremonies in which all those whose cats had died participated, and to show their grief and sorrow people were even known to shave off their eyebrows. The animal was buried just like a human being, and the owner often put some objects into the grave so that his pet could play with them in the Otherworld; even little bowls for milk have been found in the cats' cemetery.

And, of course, statues of cats were made in all sizes, showing them in different positions: often sitting proudly like a little queen, adorned with golden earrings, and some-

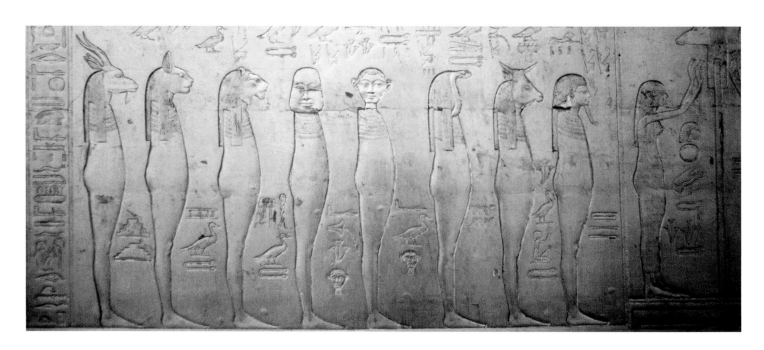

Forms of the sun-god depicted on the second shrine of Tutankhamun (1336–1327 B.C.), Egyptian Museum, Cairo

times peacefully lying down. Some of the most delightful figurines show a mother cat with some of her kittens. These statuettes, or rather, imitations of such miniature art works, still delight the tourists in the Khan al-Khalili in Cairo, as well as cat lovers who visit the shops of the major museums in Europe and the United States.

We do not know how and when the Arabs became acquainted with cats. Perhaps a Christian monk brought his furry companion from Egypt to the other shore of the Red Sea. One thing is certain, though: the Bedouins do not like cats, as becomes clear from stories and proverbs of Bedouin origin. As nomads, they did not own granaries or any place to store food; hence, there was no need for an animal that might scare away or eat the greedy mice. Rather, the *ghul*, the desert demon whose name has given us the English ghoul, was thought to appear in cat's shape to frighten the camels.

But in the urban areas of Arabia and of other countries that became Islamized in the seventh and eighth centuries, cats played an important role, and folktales abound. For example, everyone knows how, according to folk tradition, the Prophet Muhammad cut off his coat sleeve because he had to get up for prayer and was loath to disturb his cat Muizza, peacefully sleeping on the sleeve; or how a cat gave birth to her kittens on the prophet's coat, and he took care of the offspring. Therefore, numerous friendly sayings about cats are attributed to him. For the future generations of Muslims, it was essential to know that the cat is a clean animal—even if she drinks from the water in a bowl, this water

A mouse gnaws at a net entrapping a cat, hoping to enlist its aid against the owl and the weasel which threaten it. From a 14th-century copy of the Arabic manuscript 'Kalila wa Dimna,' Bodleian Library, Oxford.

can still be used for the ablutions before prayer (while the dog's saliva renders everything impure). Thus we often find cats in the mosque, and they are gladly welcomed there not only because they keep the mice at bay, but also because the pious think that the cat herself performs ablutions, while purring is often compared to the *dhikr*, the rhythmic chanting of the Sufis.

To show mercy to animals, and in particular to cats, was considered meritorious. A lovely Sufi tale tells how Shibli, an Iraqi Sufi of the tenth century, appeared to someone in a dream after his death, and recounted how God Almighty had shown mercy to him. Being interrogated by the Lord as to whether he was aware which of his acts had gained him

forgiveness, Shibli—so he told the dreaming person—had enumerated a long list of virtuous acts, supererogative prayers, travels in search of knowledge, fasting, almsgiving, and much more. "But the Lord told me: 'Not for all this have I forgiven you!' And I asked: 'But then why?' And He said: 'Do you remember that winter night in Baghdad, when it was snowing and you saw a tiny kitten shivering on a wall, and you took it and put it under your fur coat?' 'Yes, I remember that!' 'Now, because you had pity on that poor little cat, I have mercy on you.'"

It seems that from early days the Arabs kept cats as pets. Otherwise we would not understand why (according to one early history) the Prophet's young widow, A'isha, when complaining that everyone had deserted her, added: "Even the cat has left me alone."

Cats were companions of pious men and women, and they were loved by scholars not only for their beauty and elegance but also for practical purposes. Arabic poets and litterateurs wrote eulogies on their cats or described them in grand, hymnic, rhyming sentences, for they protected their precious libraries from the assault of mice. We see before us the proud tomcat, strutting through the house, "with eyes shining as though they were of colored glass," with soft long fur and "teeth like saws" (Abu Ja'far al-Ausi, twelfth century). And we read of other cats who faithfully served their master to bring him good luck (as Puss-in-Boots does in Europe), or of cats who would sacrifice themselves for the benefit of their owner, or even bring a mysterious concoction with which their owner could cure an ailing princess. Various parts of the cat—especially a black cat—could serve for magic purposes or were used in strange medications: fumigation with a wild cat's brain precipitated abortion, and if you carried some cat's teeth with you no enemy could overcome you.

A cat clearly at home with 'The married man and his family'—a scene from 'Kitab al-Bulhan,' a manuscript in a style attributed to Baghdad c. 1400. Bodleian Library, Oxford

In Cairo we find even more aspects of feline importance. Up to E. W. Lane's days the caravans of pilgrims going to the sacred precincts of Mecca took a number of cats with them, though we do not know whether this was a reminiscence of the Prophet's love of cats, or the feeling that the gentle creatures might bring good luck. Or were the pilgrims afraid lest mice and, even worse, rats might destroy whatever foodstuff the caravan carried? Whatever the reason behind this custom may have been, these Egyptian cats were looked after by a woman, the "mother of cats," who was responsible for their well-being.

Today, as the photographs which follow prove, the mystique of the cat is still very much alive in the Egyptian environment. For after all, should not the cat be important in the Muslim world, as apparently God inspired man to write the cat's name—qi,t,t in Arabic letters—in such a shape that it looks like itself?

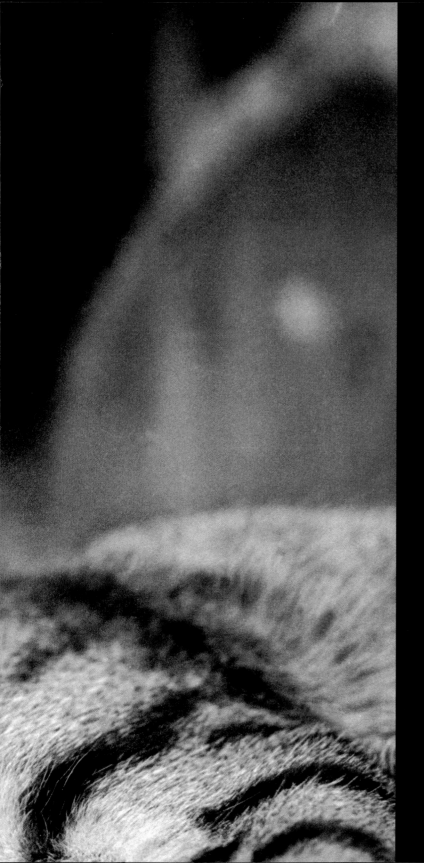

The name of the god who guards you is Cat.

Spell 145, 12th gate of the 'Book of the Dead,'
19th Dynasty (c. 1250 B.C.)

The 'Book of the Dead' was a collection of religious spells inscribed on papyrus and on the walls of tombs, which enabled the souls of ordinary people buried there to participate in the nightly journey and subsequent regeneration of the sun-god.

Mosque of al-Mu'ayyad near Bab Zuwayla

Who is this Great Tomcat?

He is the god Ra himself. He was called 'miu' when Sia spoke of him because he was mewing during what he was doing, and that was how his name of cat came into being.

spell 335, 'Coffin Texts' (c. 2000 B.C.)

'Coffin Texts' were religious spells written on the wooden coffins of ordinary people to equip them for the afterworld.

ABOVE: *A family living on the banks of the Nile near al-Manyal;* OPPOSITE: *Giza Pyramids*

Do not laugh at a cat.

'Instruction of Ankhsheshonq,'
Ptolemaic period (4th–3rd centuries B.C.)

The Egyptian Museum, Cairo

*O cat of lapis lazuli, great of forms...
mistress of the embalming house, grant
the beautiful West in peace...*

from the funerary papyrus of Espaheran (c. 900 B.C.), Bodleian Library, Oxford

Next to Naguib Mahfouz Cafe in Khan al-Khalili

W

hen a man smells of myrrh, his wife is a kitten to him. When a man is suffering, his wife is a lioness to him.

'Instruction of Ankhsheshonq,' Ptolemaic period (4th–3rd centuries B.C.)

Translator M. Depauw notes the demotic word translated here as 'kitten' may also mean 'monkey.' However, in this context, the former appears to make more sense.

Mashrabiyyah Bazaar, Khan al-Khalili

The beasts of the desert shall drink from the river of Egypt and rest on its banks because nobody shall scare them away.

from the text known as 'The Prophecies of Neferti' (c. 1980 B.C.)

ABOVE: *Outskirts of Giza near the Pyramids*
OPPOSITE: *Felucca dock in Maadi, south of downtown Cairo*

*S*he rages like the goddess
Sehkmet and she is friendly
like the goddess Bastet.

from 'The Myth of the Eye of the Sun,'
wall inscription at Philae temple (c. 150 B.C.)

OPPOSITE: *Coptic Church of St. George, Mar Girgis*
ABOVE: *Pharaonic shoe sellers, Khan al–Khalili*

O peaceful one,
who returns to peace,
you cause me to see the
darkness of your making.
Lighten me that I can perceive
your beauty, turn towards me,
O beautiful one when at peace,
the peaceful one when at peace,
the peaceful one who knows
a return to peace.

inscription on a stela (c. 1200 B.C.),
Ashmolean Museum, Oxford

A *stela* is a commemorative stone slab or gravestone.

Mosque of al–Mu'ayyad near Bab Zuwayla

Those who love cats
have a strong faith.

Turkish proverb

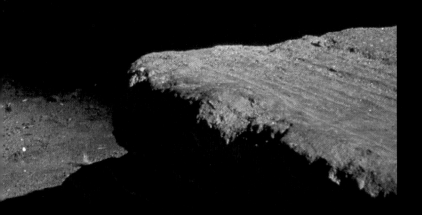

Dar al–Salam, Cairo

The yellow one from the bakery
smelled like a cream puff—
she followed us home.
We buried our faces
in her sweet fur.
One cat hid her head
while I practiced violin.
But she came out for piano.
At night she played sonatas
on my quilt.
One cat built a secret nest
in my socks.
One sat in the window
staring up at the street all day
while we were at school.
One cat loved the radio dial.
One cat almost smiled.

'Every Cat Had a Story' by Naomi Shihab Nye,
Palestinian–American writer (b. 1952)

Opposite the Mosque of Qajamas al-Ishaqi, Darb al-Ahmar

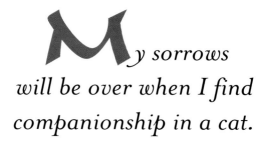

*M y sorrows
will be over when I find
companionship in a cat.*

Ahmad Ibn Faris, an Iranian scholar and philologist
(d. 1005)

ABOVE: *Mashrabiyyah Bazaar, Khan al-Khalili*
OPPOSITE: *Harit al-Suramatiya, Khan al-Khalili*

There once were two men who went to a judge about a mother cat and her kittens which they both claimed to be theirs. The judge demanded that this cat be set free between their two houses and, depending on which one of the houses she chose, this would be their master. And all the people got excited, and I got excited with them. But then the cat didn't go to either house!

oral tradition, attributed to the 9th-century Egyptian jurist Imam Shafi'i

Soda stand on Shar'ia al-Falaky, Bab al-Louk

There once was a black cat, and every night she would crawl up through a dark well from deep below the ground. Then she would shed off her catskin and go to the owner of a nearby house as a woman. They would savor the joys of love night after night until morning prayer at which time she would disappear below ground again. Every morning when he awoke he would find some money she left for him in appreciation of their time together. Through the years their friendship grew so strong that she helped his daughter go on the pilgrimage to Mecca.

Moroccan folktale

Mr. Fawzy with Bustan at Sharia Muhammad Mahmud

Rosebuds
Surrounded by thorns:
Mother cat carrying babies in mouth.

*from a poem by Jalaluddin Rumi numbered 2854
in the Divan–i Kabir, ed. B. Furuzanfar, Tehran 1957–1975*

OPPOSITE: *Mosque of Ibn Tulun*
ABOVE: *Mashrabiyyah Bazaar, Khan al-Khalili*

Т he grammarian Ibn Babshad was sitting with his friends on
the roof of a mosque in Cairo, eating some food. When a cat passed
by they gave her some morsels: she took them and ran away, only to
come back time and time again. The scholars followed her and saw
her running to an adjacent house on whose roof a blind cat was
sitting. The cat carefully placed the morsels in front of her.
Babshad was so moved by God's caring for the blind creature that
he gave up all his belongings and lived in poverty, completely
trusting in God until he died in 1067.

oral tradition, recorded in the late 14th century by the Egyptian theologian and zoologist Damiri (d. 1405)

ABOVE: Haj 'Abdu at the Mosque of al-Mu'ayyad; OPPOSITE: Mosque of al-Mu'ayyad near Bab Zuwayla

My only protection against
the cold is my shivering—
as if I'm a cat longing
for the sunshine.

anonymous Andalusian poem (c. 12th century)

When Sidi Heddi came to his dwelling in the mountains, he found the land full of vipers and scorpions. He was very afraid and asked for help from Sidi Maschisch, who sent him a white cat and ordered him to treat it with love.

custom of the Moroccan dervish order of the Heddawa, recorded by French anthropologist René Brunel in 'Le Monachisme Errant dans l'Islam: Sidi Heddi et les Heddawa,' Paris, Larose, 1955

Artist Badr Osman 'Ali Hafez and his cat near Midan Tahrir

There once was a man who had a wife who was quar-
relsome and greedy. Whatever food he brought home she
devoured, and he, being timid, rarely complained.
One day the husband brought, for a guest, a piece of meat
he had bargained fiercely for. In his absence the wife ate it
all, roasted and with wine. When he returned he asked,
"Where is the meat? The guest is here. We have to offer
him something special!"

The wife replied, "The cat ate it! Go and buy
another piece of meat for our meal!"

He exclaimed, "Oh servant, bring a balance
so I can weigh the cat!"

He weighed the cat and it weighed three pounds exactly so
the husband said to his deceitful wife, "The meat weighed
three pounds and a half while the cat, my dear, weighs
three pounds only! If this is the cat, where is the meat,
and if this is the meat, then tell me where is the cat?"

Turkish folktale, as related by Jalaluddin Rumi

Corniche al-Nil, Garden City

Love plays with my heart as a cat plays with a mouse.

Abu Nuwas, the best-known love poet of early Abbasid (late 8th-century) Baghdad

OPPOSITE: *Mish-Mish playing in Bab al-Louk*
ABOVE: *Copper shop upstairs in Khan al-Khalili*

How strange,
how strange,
how strange a tale!
A black cat, look, who has a tail!

from an anonymous Egyptian poem on alchemy, c. 12th–14th centuries

*S*he has bewitched me with her
darkness and light as she appears
to be made of ebony and ivory.

*attributed to Ibn Tabataba, 10th-century representative
of the descendants of the Prophet (sharifs) in Cairo*

ABOVE: *Road 82, Maadi*
OPPOSITE: *Brass shop in Khan al-Khalili*

The black cat used to move from one
table to the other, looking for crumbs and
little pieces of fish, loitering at the
customers' feet and rubbing against their
legs, with the idleness of one spoiled by
luxury... The customers bandied jokes
and anecdotes, and got more intimate by
expressing their complaints and grievances
to each other. Sometimes one with a clear
voice would start a merry song, so that
this damp buried place overflowed
with happiness.
"There is no harm in forgetting for
an hour or two the problems of poverty
and children."
"And forgetting the heat and flies..."
"And forgetting there is another world
outside these bars..."
"And enjoying playing with
the black cat."

from the short story 'The Tavern of the Black Cat' by Naguib Mahfouz (b. 1911)

Al-Hurriya Coffeeshop, Bab al-Louk

When a cat purrs loud in autumn, a harsh winter is on the way.

Turkish folk saying

OPPOSITE: *Near Sharia Sabri 'Abu 'Alam, Bab al-Louk*
ABOVE: *Sayyida and Basboosa on Sharia al-Mu'izz Li-Din Allah near Bab Zuwayla*

You became wild, you became a street cat!
Did you not fly around my heart like a nightingale?

No longer is your beauty a revelation,
Your face no longer a place of worship.

Your former tenderness grew coarse,
What were your fineries, became torn...

How can your beauty betray itself,
How can wine turn to quinine?

I'm afraid for you—decorated with jewelry—
And now you've become like a gypsy
prostituting herself.

An existentialist cat roaming the streets at night—
But who's still dreaming of you?

from 'Song for Mourning a Cat' by Nizar Qabbani, Syrian poet (d. 1998)

Four street cats in Bab al-Louk

Among the animals on Noah's ark there were some pigs. Noah asked them to behave and stay quiet, so as not to rock the ark. But the boar mounted the sow, and Noah hit them with a stick. The pigs snorted which brought out the mouse. The lion had just sneezed, and from his nose appeared the cat who chased after the mouse. The camel who watched all this fuss burst into such laughter that his upper lip split.

Moroccan folktale

ABOVE: *Near the Giza Pyramids*
OPPOSITE: *Old Camel Market, Imbaba*

Cat you went and didn't come back—
You were like a son to me!
Loving you so, how could we forget you?
Your youthful vigour was great,
Scarcely able to be measured.
You could chase away evils,
Protect us from snakebites and gnawing rats!
You fetched out of the house each mouse,
Whether hidden in his hole or not...
The midday glow of summer didn't frighten you,
Nor winter frost dampen your courage...
My heart shuddered in fear for your life—
You slipped in without trembling
And trod in the pigeon-house very gently,
And reached for the fledglings powerfully,
And scattered the feathers in the street—
And the tender flesh you took to eat.
The temptation to feast yourself
Sent you bloody revenge from the pigeons' master,
Just as you dealt with his pigeons.

*from 'Farewell Poem for a Deceased Cat' by Ibn al-Mu'tazz,
an Abbasid prince who was caliph for one day (d. 908)*

Poultry shop in Bab al-Louk

63

When a cat dies
it is supposed to be followed
in death by a dervish, and
the other way round. When a cat
dies unexpectedly the dervishes mourn
for her and bury her in a grave that is
in line with Mecca. They bury her and say,
"Go on my friend, may God give you peace
and peace for us." On that grave they'll
put a stone. Sometimes the dead cat
will be wrapped in a piece of
cloth, and the dervishes
will cry hot tears.

*custom of the Moroccan dervish order
of the Heddawa*

A 'dervish' is a member of an ascetic Islamic order using
special rituals to achieve communion with God.

Near the mausoleum of Sultan Qa'it Bay in the City of the Dead

64

*T*he white cat
on the white chair
lives white minutes
I'm not even in.

'Envy' by Naomi Shihab Nye

opposite: *Ramadan tenting, Dokki*
above: *Near Midan al-Hurriya, Maadi*

67

The world is differently-shaped,
wavering in strong light,
as if viewed through water.
Edges dissolve, re-form.

The cat blinks.
She has waited a long time
for you to remember her name.
Her purr, steady as the clock's heartbeat,
is a bridge from the place you have left
to the place you now are.
A reliable companion,
she guides you toward the land
whose name comes to your lips slowly.

*from 'After Fever' by Palestinian-American writer
Lisa Suhair Majaj (b. 1960)*

Mosque of al-Mu'ayyad near Bab Zuwayla

When sorrows press my heart I say:
Maybe they'll disappear one day:
When books will be my friends at night,
My darling then: the candle light,
My sweetest friend: a kitten white!

Damiri, an Egyptian theologian and zoologist (d. 1405)

OPPOSITE: *A stray kitten in an old man's hands, Darb al-Ahmar*
ABOVE: *Mr. Ibrahim and Mish-Mish on the banks of the Nile, Zamalek*

71

A cat once killed a snake that was attacking the Prophet. Grateful, Muhammad stroked her back — hence cats never fall on their backs. He also put his noble hand on her forehead and that is why every cat has four dark lines on her forehead.

tradition of the Prophet quoted by Jalaluddin Rumi (d. 1273)

Mosque of al-Mu'ayyad near Bab Zuwayla

F
**riendship between cats and dogs ends
when the butcher door opens.**

Turkish folk saying

Al-Ahram supermarket, Maadi

Snake slipped into a mosque,
"I'm fleeing from an enemy, protect me."
Hedgehog said, "Give me my prey so I
can eat." He was given liver instead.
Snake twisted around the mosque guard
intending to bite him. Another person
came to help with a bag with a cat inside.

The Prophet stroked the cat on its back
for killing the snake, and by doing so,
blessed it.

This is why the cat lands on its feet—the
cat's back, because of the touch of the
Prophet, can never strike the ground.

tradition of the Prophet quoted by Jalaluddin Rumi
(d. 1273)

In the Mosque of Ibn Tulun

After her children are married the mother occupies herself raising cats.

'Mudhakkiraat Sa'im' by Ahmad Bahgat, Egyptian writer (b.1932)

The tyranny of cats is better
than the justice of mice.

Arab folk saying

Mosque of al-Mu'ayyad near Bab Zuwayla

1 f cats had wings the sparrow would be in danger.

Persian folk saying

Mish—Mish on the banks of the Nile, Zamalek

The cat does not render you or your water for ablution impure.

oral tradition, attributed to A'isha, the wife of the Prophet

ABOVE: *Copper shop upstairs in Khan al-Khalili*
OPPOSITE: *Near Fishawi's in Sikkit Khan al-Khalili*

The month of Ramadan weighs heavily upon me. It is no longer that beautiful movement which once made me go out through love and desire for God.
. . . I remember that in my early childhood I used to fast, and at the hour when the fast ended, I would go out taking my meal with me and give it to the stray dogs and cats. Then I would break my fast with three dates, looking at the stars and feeling that inside me there were even brighter stars.

'Mudhakkiraat Sa'im' by Ahmad Bahgat, Egyptian writer (b.1932)

Inside the Tentmakers Bazaar near Bab Zuwayla

In his own house, the cat is also a lion.

Sindhi folk saying

OPPOSITE: *Sharia Al-Mu'izz Li-Din Allah, Khan al-Khalili*
ABOVE: *Near Sharia Sabri 'Abu 'Alam, Bab al-Louk*

*The cat sleeps on the sheik's lap
and on the prayer carpet is she at home.*

Persian mystic poet 'Attar (d. 1220)

ABOVE: *In front of the 'sahil' or cleansing area in the mosque of Ibn Tulun*
OPPOSITE: *In the window of the Mosque of Qajamas al-Ishaqi, Darb al-Ahmar*

1f a man sees himself in a dream looking at a large cat, it is a good omen and means that a large harvest will come to him.

from a dream book written on papyrus (c. 1250 B.C., but originally compiled perhaps as early as 1900 B.C.); Chester Beatty III recto.; British Museum

Selling olives for Ramadan on Sharia al-Mahdi, near Midan al-Opera

*I*n springtime when roses blossom, cats and nightingales seem to sing. But we know how large the difference is between the two.

folk saying from Afghanistan

ABOVE: *'Sahil' or cleansing area in the Mosque of al-Mu'ayyad near Bab Zuwayla*
OPPOSITE: *Outside a wedding shop in Ataba*

94

قطا